HOW TO CARE FOR YOUR NEW PET

CARING FOR
MY NEW
MOUSE

John Bankston

Mitchell Lane

PUBLISHERS

2001 SW 31st Avenue
Hallandale, FL 33009
www.mitchelllane.com

First Edition, 2021.

Author: John Bankston
Designer: Ed Morgan
Editor: Morgan Brody

Names/credits:
Title: Caring for My New Mouse / by John Bankston
Description: Hallandale, FL : Mitchell Lane Publishers

Series: How to Care for Your New Pet

Library bound ISBN: 978-1-58415-162-3

eBook ISBN: 978-1-58415-165-4

Photo credits: Freepik.com, Shutterstock

CONTENTS

Words in **bold** throughout can
be found in the Glossary.

Mouse in the House

Pet mice are cute, small, inexpensive, and **popular** with children, especially since they are exposed to them in animated movies, books, and TV shows.

But not everyone thinks mice are nice. Some people are afraid of them. Dogs, cats, and snakes can hunt them. Not every family wants a mouse in their house.

Yet mice have been pets for **centuries**. In the 1800s, they became a favorite pet in Europe.

Pet mice are easy to tame. They can be taught tricks. Some will come when you call. They make for low-maintenance **companions** with a lot of personality. Pet mice can be handled but they are **fragile** and should be treated gently. Children caring for them should always be supervised by an adult. Before getting one, learn all you can about having a pet mouse in your house.

DID YOU KNOW?

Mice can have up to 150 babies a year.

Mouse Facts

There are hundreds of types of mice. Common varieties include the deer mouse, house mouse, field mouse, wood mouse, dormouse, spiny mouse, and zebra mouse. Mice are everywhere!

A mouse is a rodent. Guinea pigs, gerbils, and rats are also rodents. These animals have strong teeth that never stop growing. Mouse owners sometimes get their pet's teeth trimmed.

The most common pet mouse is the house mouse. The house mouse is from Asia. Traveling on boats, house mice spread across the world.

The house mouse lives near people. They are **nocturnal**. This means they like to sleep during the day and come out at night.

Mice, unlike cats and dogs, can move their whiskers to map out their surroundings, much as humans use their fingers to feel around in a darkened room. Their whiskers also help them judge if a hole is big enough.

Most pet mice are house mice. A mouse weighs about two ounces.

They are around half-a-foot long, including the tail. This is about the length of most adults' hands. The tail is as long as the body. A mouse uses its tail for balance, allowing it to travel along very narrow wires and ropes.

DID YOU KNOW?

Mice have poor vision, but excellent hearing. They are also colorblind.

Setting Up Your Mouse House

Before you get your mouse, set up its house. *Don't wait*! Make the little guy's first night at your home safe and comfy.

The mouse's home is its **habitat**. You will be creating a habitat for your pet mouse. Pet mice spend most of their lives in their cage, so it needs to be large enough to be a complete environment for them, with enough space and furnishings to allow your pet to feel comfortable, secure and safe.

The best mouse cages give your pet plenty of room to play. There are three different types of housing to choose from. Glass **aquariums** with tight-fitting mesh tops are strong and make it easy to see what your mouse is up to. Keep in mind they may be heavy to move around and may be costly. Plastic cages are inexpensive and lightweight, but some mice can chew escape holes in the plastic. Metal or wire cages provide for air flow and the ability to pass food through the bars without removing the lid. But some mice like to gnaw on the bars. Avoid wooded cages.

Cages that are one-foot tall, one-foot wide and one-and-one-half feet long are fine. Bigger is always better. More room means you can put more fun things in the cage for playtime.

Wire hurts mice feet. Some cages have a solid floor. Or use a mat. Scatter paper across the bottom. Use paper without ink. Tear the paper into strips. *Avoid pine or cedar shavings. These can make your mouse sick.*

Place a nesting box in one corner. A clean plastic food container works well. Tear up some white tissues and put them in the container. This will be your mouse's bed.

On the other end, place a food bowl. Use porcelain or ceramic. Your mouse won't chew them up. They are easy to clean. Mice spill when they drink from a dish. Use a water bottle. It should clip to the side of the cage. Hang it at mouse height. Glass or metal bottles are best. Plastic bottles get chewed.

Mice are escape artists. A tightly secured lid on whatever type of cage you get is a must!

After you get your mouse, keep its cage clean. Remove most dirty paper. Leave a bit behind. This helps mice feel safe. Keep their food dish and water bottle clean. Avoid lemon scented dish soap.

Once a week, put your mouse in its critter keeper. Remove all the paper. Use a pet-safe cleaner. Have an adult help.

Mice love to crawl through paper towel tubes. They also like small empty boxes. Their favorite exercise is spinning. They don't ride a bike! They run on a wheel. Find a wheel that is a good size for your mouse. Mice need to run without having to bend. Because their feet or tail can get caught in wire, choose a wheel that is solid.

DID YOU KNOW?

Male mice are called bucks. Females are does.
A baby mouse is called a "pinky." A group of
mice is called a "mischief."

13

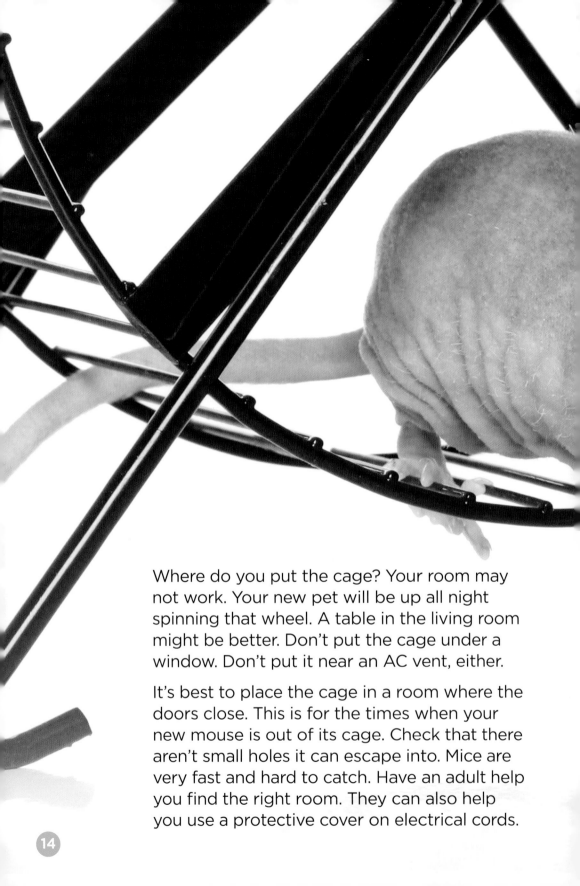

Where do you put the cage? Your room may not work. Your new pet will be up all night spinning that wheel. A table in the living room might be better. Don't put the cage under a window. Don't put it near an AC vent, either.

It's best to place the cage in a room where the doors close. This is for the times when your new mouse is out of its cage. Check that there aren't small holes it can escape into. Mice are very fast and hard to catch. Have an adult help you find the right room. They can also help you use a protective cover on electrical cords.

Mice love to chew and chewing these cords is very dangerous. You'll also want to move any plants.

Once you've set up the house, it's time to get the mouse.

Getting Your Mouse

Buying a mouse isn't like getting other pets. Places selling mice must do one thing well. They must keep boy mice away from girl mice. A female mouse can give birth when she is two months old. Bringing a mouse home that is about to be a mom can be very hard.

Look around the pet store. Are the cages clean? The mice need room to play. The mouse should have a smooth **coat**. The ears and tail should be pink and clean. It should have a lot of energy.

Dog shows put dogs on display. "Fancy mice" have their own shows. Judges pick the best mice. They judge their colors, coats and behavior. These mice can be white, brown or gold. There are even blue mice! The mice must have big ears and big eyes. They have long tails and pink or brown eyes.

Breeders raise fancy mice. They do cost more. But breeders are good at separating boys from girls. They hand tame them. Make sure the mice are clean. They should not be in crowded cages. Your local animal shelter might also have mice for **adoption**.

Female mice are easier to raise. They usually smell better, too! Mice are **social**. They don't like being alone. Two females will be very happy. Boy mice usually fight. Owners say two mice are twice as nice.

DID YOU KNOW?

It is a myth that mice love cheese. Because of their sensitive sense of smell, mice even shy away from certain types of cheese.

Mouse Play

Not playing with a new pet right away is difficult. Your mouse needs time. Training is about trust. Let your mouse get to know you.

When you are near its cage, speak softly. Move slowly. Only open the cage to change the water and food. After a few days, give it a treat. Push it partway into the cage. If it comes to you, give it the treat.

Once it comes for the treat, start putting your hand through the open cage door. Let the mouse take the treat from your hand. Never try to lower your hand onto a mouse. They might see that as an attack.

Rest your hand palm up inside a cage. Put a treat on it. Mice love to climb. Let it climb onto your hand. You can also put the treat onto your wrist. This will make it want to climb onto your hand. You may want to say "treat." This lets it know a treat is coming.

Again, take your time. It might take weeks. When it is used to getting on your hand, you can give it a scratch. Scratch its sides and back of its head. This is a lot like how mice **groom** each other.

You are taming your mouse. There are two ways to pick it up. Shy mice might like climbing into a cup. Put the cup in its cage. Turn it on its side. Put a treat in the cup. When it gets inside, very gently put it right side up. Cover the cup with one hand while picking it up with the other.

DID YOU KNOW?

When mice are threatened by something, they play dead until they feel danger has passed.

Bolder mice can be carried on the palm of your hand. Hold the **scruff** on the back of its neck. This keeps your mouse from running away. You can also hold onto the tail. Use the base of the tail. Never hold the mouse by the tip of its tail. It can get hurt.

Never squeeze your mouse. You should sit down when you hold the mouse. Mice can be squirmy. They get hurt when they are dropped.

Always wash your hands before and after playtime. Mice can get colds from people. Go slow. You will soon have a mouse that wants to play all the time!

Meals for Mice

Food is the best way to befriend your mouse. Give it treats he likes. Soon he will look forward to the time you spend together. In the wild, mice eat all sorts of things. Like most people, mice are **omnivores**.

Pet mice get bored. They don't like eating the same thing every day. Give it some **variety**.

Mice pellets can be the main meal. You can also use hamster food. There are also mixes sold at pet stores made up of grains or seeds. Make sure they aren't just eating a little.

Mice love people food. If you have spaghetti or other pasta for dinner, save some for your mouse. It should be cooked and sauce free. Whole grain crackers or bread are good, too. Remember, mice are little. Do not overfeed your mouse. A piece of a cracker is more than enough.

A thumbnail size bit of peanut butter is great. Too much can make them choke! A few sunflower seeds are good, too.

Mice also love apples, strawberries, carrots and salad greens. Have an adult help you wash and chop. Every mouse is different. They won't like everything you give them. Remove uneaten food daily.

Never give your mouse junk food. Cookies, candy and chips are bad for mice. Chocolate can be deadly. Never, ever give your mouse chocolate.

Fresh water is very important. Feed your mice well and you will have a healthy, happy pet.

DID YOU KNOW?

Pets are getting heavier. A study showed cats and dogs weigh more today than ever before. Mice and rats have gained weight, too.

Vet Time

Pet mice often come with a surprise. Babies! Mice have more unplanned **litters** than other pets. If your mouse has babies, leave her alone! Stay away from the cage. You should only open the cage for food, water and nesting paper. Do not try to touch the babies or the new mom.

It will take a few weeks before she will let you pick her up again. Use that time to find homes for the babies. Baby mice can be adopted when they are two months old.

You will want to see a **veterinarian** when you get your mouse. Veterinarians are doctors for animals. Not every vet takes care of mice. Find one that does. The vet will help you make sure your mouse is a boy or a girl. They will help with its teeth, too.

Do your part to help keep your mouse healthy. Notice if he doesn't want to eat or play. If your pet has trouble breathing, this is another sign. Taking your pet to the vet early can make a difference. You will want to spend time with your mouse. They are fun to play with and to watch. This is why mice are such a popular pocket pet.

SHOPPING LIST

This is a list of some things your mouse will need:

☐ A glass, plastic or metal cage at least one-foot tall, one-foot wide, and one-and-one-half feet long

☐ Mouse food and treats (hamster food is okay for mice)

☐ White paper towels or tissues

☐ Glass water bottle and ceramic food bowl

☐ Solid plastic, large wheel

☐ Hideaway place (small box or container with shredded paper)

☐ Toys including cardboard paper towel or tissue rolls

☐ Wood fruit for chewing (sold in the bird section of pet stores)

☐ Hemp rope for climbing

☐ A critter keeper to bring them home

FIND OUT MORE

Online
There are several sites that will help you raise a healthy and happy mouse:

The Animal Humane Society offers advice on mouse care:
https://www.animalhumanesociety.org/adoption/mouse-care

The American Fancy Rat and Mouse Association (AFRMA) have information on breeders and raising "fancy mice:"
http://www.afrma.org

They also offer information on care:
Royer, Nichole. "Kids's Guide to Basic Pet Rat & Mouse Care,"AFRMA. April 1, 2016. http://www.afrma.org/kidsguide.htm

Petfinder connects people with adoptable animals. They even have a section for "small and furry" animals like mice.
https://www.petfinder.com/search/small-furry-for-adoption/us

Learn how to hand tame your mouse:
http://youtu.be/D2PXAEoEGIA

Learn some tricks to teach your mouse:
http://youtu.be/MRh4weM19qc

Books

Alderton, David. *Looking After Small Pets.* London: Southwater 2012.

Little, Ben. *Pet Mice: Your Pet Mouse.* Happy Care Guide Sussex, UK: World Ideas Ltd. 2014.

Thomas, Isabel. *Squeak's Guide to Caring for Your Pet Rats or Mice.* Portsmouth,NH: Heinemann. 2014.

Schuetz, Kari. *Mice.* Minneapolis, MN :Bellwether Media. 2014.

GLOSSARY

adoption
Taking care of someone without a family

aquarium
Glass tank for fish, reptiles and some small animals

breeders
People who keep or take care of animals in order to produce similar ones

century
100 years

companion
A person or animal you spend time with

coat
The outer covering of fur, hair, or wool on an animal

fragile
Easily broken or damaged

groom
Clean and care for

habitat
Natural home of an animal

litters
Group of young animals born at the same time

nocturnal
Awake and active at night

omnivores
Eating meat, vegetables and many other food

popular
Liked or enjoyed by many people

scruff
Skin on the back of the neck

social
Comfortable playing and being around others

variety
Choices or selection of things, like food

veterinarian
Doctor who specializes in animal care

BIBLIOGRAPHY

Kruzer, RVT, LVT. Adrienne. "Monitoring and Managing Overgrown Mice Teeth." *The Spruce Pets*. February 17, 2017. https://www.thesprucepets.com/mouse-teeth-1238479

McLeod, DVM. Lianne. "Breeding Data for Fancy Mice." *The Spruce Pets*. February 15, 2017. https://www.thesprucepets.com/breeding-data-for-fancy-mice-1238491

"Can You Litter Train Mice?" *The Spruce Pets*. January 8, 2019. https://www.thesprucepets.com/litter-training-pet-mice-1238484

"Choosing and Caring for a Pet Mouse." *The Spruce Pets*. May 5, 2019. https://www.thesprucepets.com/choosing-and-caring-for-pet-mice-1236741

"Do Mice Make Good Pets for Kids?" *The Spruce Pets*. May 5, 2019. https://www.thesprucepets.com/do-mice-make-good-pets-1238485

"How to Find a Veterinarian for Your Exotic Pet." *The Spruce Pets*. July 28, 2017. https://www.thesprucepets.com/veterinarian-for-your-exotic-pet-1237279

"How to Train Your Mouse to Play with You." *The Spruce Pets*. May 4, 2019. https://www.thesprucepets.com/taming-and-handling-pet-mice-1238481

"Top 10 Toys for Mice." *The Spruce Pets*. February 17, 2017. https://www.thesprucepets.com/top-toys-for-mice-1238494

"What to Do If Your Mouse Has Babies." *The Spruce Pet*s. November 25, 2018. https://www.thesprucepets.com/my-mouse-had-babies-what-should-i-do-1238486

"Mouse Care Guide." *VetBabble*. January 22, 2019. https://www.vetbabble.com/small-pets/mice/

"Porky pets." *WR News*. January 28, 2011.

Quesenberry, DVM, MPH, DABVP (Avian). Katherine E. "Introduction to Mice." *MSD Vet Manual*. https://www.msdvetmanual.com/all-other-pets/mice/introduction-to-mice

INDEX

ABOUT THE AUTHOR

John Bankston

The author of over 100 books for young readers, John Bankston lives in Miami Beach, Florida with his rescue dog Astronaut. He loved learning about how friendly and tame pet mice can be.